P9-CFM-411

"Of all the means of expression, photography is the only one that fixes forever the precise and transitory instant."

Henri Cartier-Bresson

For
Liz Tockman,
the beach ball tosser

Designed by Bruce McMillan
Text set in ITC Kabel
Color separations by Color Dot Graphics, Inc.
Printed on 80 lb Warrenflo
First edition printed and bound
by Horowitz / Rae

Quote by Henri Cartier-Bresson
from *The Decisive Moment,* 1952,
courtesy of Simon & Schuster, Inc.

Copyright © 1992 by Bruce McMillan
All rights reserved
Printed in the United States of America
First Edition

Library of Congress
Cataloging-in-Publication Data
McMillan, Bruce.
Beach ball—left, right / by Bruce McMillan.
p.   cm.
Summary: Introduces the concept
of "left" and "right"
as the reader follows the airborne travels
of a colorful beach ball.
ISBN 0-8234-0946-5
1. Left and right (Psychology)—Juvenile literature.
[1. Left and right.]   I. Title.
BF637.L36M36 1992 91-32802   CIP   AC
152.3'35—dc20

Beach Ball - Left, Right

conceived and
photo-illustrated by
Bruce McMillan

Holiday House / **New York**

left

right

left

right

left

right

left

left

left

right

left

right

right

left

right

left

right

left

Learning Left and Right

"Left and right" is an important concept for children to learn and master. It applies to reading, writing, following directions, giving directions, and something as simple as greeting a friend with a handshake.

This book introduces children to left and right through a concept story. In addition to determining which side of the photo the beach ball is on, children will learn that their left hand is holding the left page of the book, and their right hand is holding the right page of the book. Once children master left and right from this viewpoint, they will be able to apply what they've learned to the world around them, expanding on their new skill.

Making This Book

I photo-illustrated this book near my home in York County, Maine. The people, animals, and places appearing with the beach ball are, in order of appearance: Christopher "the beach baller" Gamble, Chris "the painter" Stavros, Aussie "the dog" McNally, Thomas "the line worker" McDonough, the Vendituoli family's "fenced" barn, the Ridley family's "curious" Hereford cows, Paul "the pointing Sanford firefighter" Morrison, Todd "the turning Sanford firefighter" Levesque, Ruth "the left bench sitter" Batt, and Richard "the right bench sitter" Batt.

The beach ball really was — as it appears in the photos — in midair. I used a Nikon F4 camera with 85mm AF and 180mm AF lenses, and circular polarizing filters. The lighting was cloudless sunlight. The film used was Kodachrome 64, processed by Kodalux.

While shooting, we had a "ball"!

Bruce McMillan

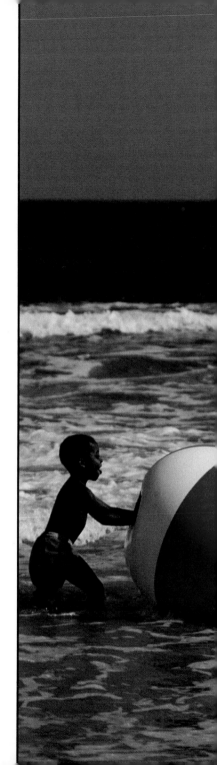